Pan Am:

A History of the Airline that Define An Age

By Don Harris

Golgotha Press

www.golgothapress.com

Table of Contents

Introduction

Pan Am (formally Pan American World Airways) was the primary international aircraft carrier for the United States for the better part of the 20th century. While not the first American passenger airline or its most successful domestically, Pan Am became the airline that was most associated with the United States in the world's eyes.

The life and story of Pan Am is tied to that of its founder, Juan Tripp, who originally founded the company to handle air mail and passenger service between Florida and Cuba. The company is credited with many innovations in the aircraft industry (including jet aircrafts, jumbo jets and the use of computer systems to handle reservations). Just as important is the company's place in pop culture and American Lore.

It was the aircraft that brought the Beatles to America and was the airliner Stanley Kubrick had in mind when he filmed the movie 2001: A Space Odyssey. Its airplanes, logo and company have appeared in movies as diverse as Blade Runner to National Lampoon's European Vacation.

In many ways, the story of Pan Am is the story of America, as the company itself became the representation to the world of America. The story includes monopolies and betrayals, innovation and competition, first class service and terrible losses. The US government aided the company at its outset, and then turned its back on it at its end. Pan Am's demise was tragic, as international forces beyond its control led to a series of mistakes, mismanagement and bad investments, that eventually brought it under.

Chapter 1: Company Beginnings

Juan Trippe was a former navy pilot who in the 1920s had attempted to start a charter service to fly wealthy New England passengers to Florida. While that venture was eventually aborted, Trippe's interest in the aviation field never waned. Instead, his focus shifted to the Caribbean and Latin America markets (as we shall see, he was not alone in this idea). With the financial backing of Cornelius Vanderbilt Whitney and William A. Rockefeller (and $250,000 raised in capital from an initial stock offering), Trippe formed the Aviation Corporation of America on June 2, 1927. The corporation was to offer air services into the Caribbean from America.

At the time, Trippe's newly formed company faced competition from two other airlines, both of whom had been formed the same year as Trippe's. One was headed by Richard Hoyt, a New York Broker who founded the Atlantic, Gulf and Caribbean Airways. The second was run by Major Henry H. "Hap" Arnold. He had formed it as a check against the expansion of German-run airlines in Columbia. He called his company Pan American Airways.

Each of the companies had assets that the other two both found attractive and, in the long run, desperately needed. Arnold's company had been awarded the contract to deliver mail to Cuba (the US government itself recognizing the need to curb German expansion).

What the company did not have were planes, money or landing rights with the Cuban government. Hoyt's airline had good financial position, and Trippe had the landing rights into Havana. To gain a share of Pan Am Trippe and Hoyt offered Arnold the assets he needed to fulfill his contract. Hoyt supplied capital while Trippe offered his landing rights. Trippe even provided Pan Am with an airplane. On October 19, 1927, Pan Am flew its first flight, delivering mail from Key West into Havana. A little over a week later, regular service between the two cities began.

The Foreign Air Mail Act

In 1928, the United States Congress passed the Foreign Air Mail Act. The act, a show of strong support for mail delivery between North and South America by the United States, regulated the international service. At the end of March, in the same year, the Postmaster General of the United States invited companies to bid on mail routes all across Latin America and the Caribbean.

This provided an impetus for Trippe, Hoyt and Arnold to come together to form one company, as each was too small to adequately handle the requirements of the bids. With Trippe taking the lead, the three companies united to form Aviation Corporation of the Americas on June 23, 1928. Trippe and his company owned 40 percent of the stock in the new company, while Hoyt was named its chairman. The subsidiary of this company became Pan American Airways.

With the former competitors' resources now combined, Pan American Airways won the bid for the mail routes. The US government began to take a vested interest in Pan Am, as they were eager to have the airline thrive. As stated before, America was wary of Germany.

The United States feared that SCADTA (the German airline) would have no competition in its routes between Latin America and the US. Having a successful American competitor, therefore, became an imperative goal for the United States. As such, the US government sought to help Pan Am wherever they could. This included pushing for a monopoly in the air and mail service for Pan Am. The United States sought to insulate the new company from American competition, to ensure the success of the airliner.

Pan Am was awarded every foreign mail route that the US government bid out, as the US wanted to make certain that only airlines capable of operating on a scale and manner that would project the pride of the United States in Latin America would be granted. As Pan Am proved itself to be both a professional company and a good ambassador for the United States, the company won more routes. In all, in addition to Havana, Cuba, Pan Am begun operating to San Juan, Puerto Rico; the Bahamas; Mexico City; and Chile. With the additional workload, (and the additional capital that was brought in) Pan Am began to expand.

Throughout the rest of the decade, and early into the next, Pan Am extended itself in Central and South America. The expansion was done through acquisitions. Trippe, now heading up the company, would purchase ailing or defunct airlines in the region, and then negotiate with the postal officials about exclusive rights (part of the Foreign Air Mail Act required that successful bidders had to have been invited for operations in the countries of Latin America). Such acquisitions included the West Indian Aerial Express (acquired in December 1928) and the Compañia Mexicana de Aviación (CMA), a Mexican-American airline (acquired in January 1929).

Trippe next set his sights on Buenos Aires, the largest city in Southern America. Competing for this city was the Grace shipping company. Eventually, the two airlines joined forces, creating the Pan American-Grace Airways to handle mail into and out of the city.

The Expansion Continues

In April 1929, Pan Am reached an agreement with United Aircraft and Transport Corporation (UATC). The agreement had UATC take a large stake in shares of Pan Am. In exchange, Pan Am agreed to only operate south of the US-Mexican border.

In September 1929, Trippe toured Latin America with Charles Lindbergh to continue Pan Am's growth. The two negotiated landing rights in a number of countries. Included on this trip was Columbia, SCADTA's main country of operations. At the end of the year, Pan Am was offering service along the west coast of South America (all the way up to Peru). In 1930, Pan Am purchased the New Yoro, Rio and Buenos Aires Line (known at NYRBA) to continue its development in the region.

Rising Stock

Pan Am's meteoric rise and aggressive expansion made it one of the hottest stocks on the New York Stock Exchange. At a time, when speculation was running rampant (speculation that in time would lead to the stock market crash of 1929), Pan Am stock would trade vehemently each time it was awarded a new route. Speculation and trading in the stock was so vociferous that, in a single day in March, 1929, the stock rose 50% in value.

Chapter 2: The Clipper Era

As air travel was in its relative infancy, many cities did not have airports (let alone runways) to handle take offs and landings. To overcome this, airlines utilized flying boat airliners (planes that could take off and land in the water). The advantage of such planes is obvious: with scarce runways in major cities international airliners could land and take off in any city that had a sheltered harbor. Pan Am was no exception. Its planes, nicknamed Clippers, provided service to all of the destinations it operated in.

The Name "Clipper"

At the time, Pan Am was competing with ocean travel. Juan Trippe decided to call his ships clippers, in an effort to associate them with the ocean liners that his passengers were used to traveling by. This was, after all, what the public was most comfortable in traveling in, especially when Pan Am begun offering service across the Atlantic.

Clipper Design

The Clippers that Pan Am used had a different design then the design of planes today. As stated before, this was due to the fact that the planes landed and took off in the water. Instead of having wings that protruded from the sides of the plane, the wings for the Pan Am Clippers went above the body of the ship.

The wings had propellers attached to them (two per side). As with today's plans, the cockpit was located in front of the ship, with the body of the ship holding the passengers. At the ships back was a tail, with wings on it to aid its flight.

Pan Am's Clippers

In total, Pan Am had four types of clippers that it used during this time: the Sikorsky S-40, the Sikorsky S-42, the Martin M-130, and the Boeing B-314. The S-40 was the first Pan Am Clipper, introduced in 1931. Its next generation, the S-42, streamlined the design of the ship, which allowed for routes across the Atlantic and Pacific Ocean.

The Martin M-130 was used primarily for its Pacific Routes (thus called the China Clipper). Finally, the apex of flying boat design was achieved in 1939 with the introduction of the Boeing B-314. Called the Yankee or Dixie Clipper, the ship was the first to have heavier-than-air passenger service across the Atlantic Ocean.

The Clipper's Flight Crews

Key to Pan Am's success was the proficiency of its flight crew. To ensure quality, the crews were rigorously trained in various forms of flying. They learned how to handle long distance routes, seaplane anchorage and berthing operations. They learned how to navigate the planes in water and how to handle the radio. Pilots were trained in aircraft repair, and the crew learned of how to handle and interpret marine tides.

The crew learned how to fly no matter the time of day or weather conditions. For day flights, they navigated utilizing the compass while judging drift from sea currents. For nighttime flights, the crews used celestial navigation. In times of difficult weather, pilots utilized dead reckoning and timed turns. For fogged-in harbors landings were done at sea, with the pilots taxiing the plane into the harbor.

Pan Am pilots knew more than just how to fly the plan. Many had merchant marine certifications and radio licenses, in addition to the pilot certificates they received. Becoming a Pan Am pilot was a lengthy process. They typically would have to work their way up, from radio operators and mechanics. As such, they were able to complete all the tasks associated with the operation of the clipper planes.

Pan Am's mechanics and support staff received similar training. Utilizing mentors, Pan Am paired new hires with experienced mechanics. Understanding how bad the conditions could potentially be, mechanics trained how to maintain and overhaul the aircrafts in harsh seaborne environments. Crews would sometimes fly spare parts to planes stranded overseas, performing the repairs themselves.

Chapter 3: Transatlantic flights

Since its inception Pan American had always wanted to get into the Atlantic commercial market. The reasons were purely financial. It was one of the most heavily traveled routes at the time. 1925 alone had a million passengers cross between Europe and America via ocean liners. Just as important was the amount of mail and express packages that traveled over the Atlantic Ocean.

After the company's success in Latin America, it next set its sights on Europe. For the transatlantic flights, Pan Am hoped to undertake, newer clippers were going to be needed that could hold more fuel and thus travel greater distances (this need resulted in the S-42 and M-130 airplanes).

Pan Am made other investments for this route across the Atlantic (inclusive of the purchase of landing rights in Iceland). The company, though, faced resistance in Europe. This frustrated Pan Am, as the company had to sit by and watch German Zeppelins (including the Hindenburg) begin regular passenger service between Europe and America.

Resistance from Europe

Pan Am faced resistance from a number of countries. Britain did not want America to have a monopoly on transatlantic service. As such, they refused to grant landing rights to Pan Am, either in Britain or British-controlled lands. Portugal frustrated the company by not allowing landing routes in Azores or Lisbon. An agreement Pan Am with Norway fell apart, due in part to British resistance.

A potential partnership with France's state airliner, Aéropostale, to start transatlantic service met resistance as the airliner, because of its operations in Latin America, viewed Pan Am as a competitor and thus decided not to team with it (and provide it profits in the transatlantic market).

It was with England that Pan Am felt it had its best bet of reaching some sort of deal. In negotiations with Great Britain, one thing became abundantly clear to Pan Am: the British sought reciprocity and parity with Pan Am. It would not grant landing rights in its country unless its airline (Imperial Airways) enjoyed the same rights in America.

In 1936, a compromise was reached. Pan Am and Imperial Airways signed an agreement that divided the route between the two. The agreement worked to eliminate competition from airlines of other countries, giving the two a monopoly for air travel between America and Britain. With this achieved reciprocity, it did not achieve parity. Imperial Airways did not yet possess the airplanes needed for transatlantic flights. As such, the agreement also stated that service would not start until both airlines were able to perform the flights. As Britain was behind in flying boat technology, Pan Am had to wait three long years before it could begin service.

Pan American Service to Bermuda

The first step in creating a reciprocal British-American transatlantic service occurred when service between the United States and Bermuda (at the time a British-held land) was opened up. On May 25, 1937, the Imperial Airways flying boat Cavalier, and Pan American's S-42B Bermuda Clipper, left Bermuda and Port Washington respectively, with each heading to the opposite airport. Regular service for both companies began in earnest a month later, on June 18, 1937.

Surveying the Atlantic – 1937

As an agreement between Pan Am and Britain had been reached (and as Pan Am waited for her British counterpart to catch up to it), Pan Am begun testing differing routes for its transatlantic route. In 1937, a Pan American S-42B flew from New York to Shediac and back. Another flight to Gander followed.

By July of that year, Imperial Airways and Pan American made the first reciprocal test flights across the Atlantic Ocean. Soon a flight route was determined to cross the Atlantic (as the planes at the time did not yet attain the needed speed or have large enough fuel tanks to make the flight directly, routes needed to be determined where the flying ships could land and refuel).

Despite the agreement, the British resisted regular service. They still did not have a plane capable of making the flight. With the Hindenburg disaster in May of that year, the British did not feel a rush to get into the market (the disaster had eliminated airships as a competitor in the transatlantic air flight market). Pan Am was forced to continue its wait.

The First Transatlantic Flights

By 1939, British technology had caught up with Pan Am. Finally for Pan Am, the first transatlantic flight was undertaken on May 20, 1939 (twelve years to the day after Charles Lindbergh had crossed the Atlantic on the Spirit of St. Louis). Pan American's B-314 Yankee Clipper left Port Washington New York and headed across the Atlantic towards Marseilles, France.

The initial flight carried 112,574 pieces of mail (mostly from stamp collectors who wanted their stamps to be a part of the first flight), four dozen California marigolds for Britain's Queen Mary, and 17 Pan Am employees. The ship flew from New York to the Azores to Marseilles, France. A month later, the Yankee Clipper took the northern route over the Atlantic, flying from New York to New Brunswick to Newfoundland to Ireland to England. The era of transatlantic flights for Pan Am had begun.

Passenger Service

Later that same month, on June 28, 1939, the Dixie Clipper left New York for France. The 22 passengers, who paid anywhere from $375 (one way) to $675 (round trip) for a ticket, had stopovers in Horta and Lisbon before finally reaching Marseilles. The next month, the Yankee Clipper began the first passenger route to England.

The Transpacific Routes

As Pan Am was waiting for the politics of air travel to play out in Europe, it turned its eyes to the Pacific Ocean. While not the original goal of the company, because of the money invested in trans-oceanic airliners (the company began investing in the airliners while negotiating with Europe), Pan Am needed to find an ocean to cross. With that in mind, it turned its attention west, to the troubles of a transpacific crossing.

The Challenge of the Pacific

Compared to the Pacific, the Atlantic crossing was very short. Routes over water for the Atlantic Ocean were less than 500 miles. Even a direct route from Newfoundland to Ireland (one leg of the northern most Atlantic route) was less than 2,000 miles. For the Pacific, the distance to San Francisco to Hawaii was 2,400 miles, and the leg from Midway to Guam was either farther. As Pan Am had not flown any leg of its travel more than 600 miles, this was a large obstacle for the company and its airplanes (and pilots) to overcome.

To deal with the distance between Midway and Guam, Trippe needed to find an island to stopover on. In his extensive research of the area, he discovered a small island called Wake. Claimed by America in 1899, it was a deserted island that had been virtually forgotten by America. But for purposes of transpacific travel, it was perfectly situated for Trippe.

The Route to China

With Wake Island, Pan Am had a path across the Pacific. Its clippers would take off from San Francisco, fly to Honolulu, on to Midway, then to Wake, with a stopover in Guam, and finally on to Manila. Having identified the route, Pan Am next went about building up the facilities for each leg of its journey. The work involved required more than just securing landing areas.

Pan Am had to develop prefabricated hotels and support buildings, especially for the abandoned island of Wake. It shipped construction equipment and long-distance direction-finding equipment to the islands. Finally, it sent a four month supply of food, 250,000 gallons of aviation fuel, and about 120 laborers, engineers, demolition experts.

Pacific Survey Flights

While the bases for the stopovers were constructed, Pan Am begun making survey flights in 1935. Pan Am was forced to fly stripped down versions of its S-42s (the ships that would eventually make this run with larger fuel tanks, the M-130s, were still not built yet). On one such survey, Pan Am became the first airliner to bring mail back from Asia to San Francisco.

Pan Am was always pushing the envelope. Less than six weeks after taking delivery of its first M-130, nicknamed the China Clipper, Pan Am prepared for regular service from San Francisco to Manila.

The China Clipper

On November 22, 1935, the China Clipper departed San Francisco on the first transpacific mail flight. After six days, five stopovers, and nearly 60 hours in the air, the China Clipper landed in Manila. Transpacific airfare had begun, and Pan Am was the company that had brought it to the world.

A year later, Pan Am was ready to transport the first paying passengers from San Francisco to Manila. On October 7, 1936, the China Clipper departed from San Francisco for Manila with its first passengers (including Pan Am employees). Two weeks later Pan Am transported the first paying airliner passengers ever across the Pacific. The cost for a ticket to Manila was $950.00.

Pan Am begun expanding its operations even further. Routes to New Zealand were added. It partnered with China National Aviation (a Chinese government-owned airline) to begin flights in China. In 1941 service expanded to Singapore. The service was run semi-monthly and reduced travel time between San Francisco and Singapore from 25 days to six.

Chapter 4: Tragedy Strikes

In 1938, the Samoan Clipper departed for a flight to Kingman Reed, Pago Pago, and Auckland. About an hour after departing Pago Pago the ship suffered an oil leak. Not willing to risk the flight, the crew decided to return to Pago Pago. However, the ship was too heavy to land there (as it still had all the fuel it needed for the long trip). The ship's captain, Captain Musick, decided to dump the fuel to allow for a landing. While dumping the fuel, the gasoline ignited. The Samoan Clipper exploded, killing the entire crew of seven aviators.

Pan Am temporarily suspended its service to New Zealand (beginning trips again in the summer of 1939 with its sturdy Boeing B-314 clippers for the trip and with an agreement with Britain to use Canton Island as an intermediate base). Still, it could not avoid tragedy. On a trip from Guam to Manila, later that same year, the Hawaiian Clipper disappeared. To date, no account has been made as to where the ship went (though conspiracy theories include that the ship was hijacked by the Imperial Japanese Navy).

Service Aboard the Clippers

The Clippers became the only American passenger aircraft of the 1930s and 1940s capable of intercontinental travel. As its main competition was ocean liners, the clippers began to offer some of the services passengers were used to receiving on the ships. The airline offered first class seats on its trips. The in-flight service crew's attire became more formal. They began wearing naval-style uniforms and adopted a set procession when boarding the aircraft.

The introduction of the Boeing 314 flying boats in 1939 improved service for Pan Am. The company was able to begin offering weekly transatlantic passenger and air mail service between England and the United States. The route took the plan from New York to Shediac, then on to Botwood, then to Foynes, and finally on to Southampton. The cost to a passenger was $375, which equates in today's dollars to about $5,300.

The Outbreak of World War II

In 1940, Pan Am and TWA began using the Boeing 307 Stratoliner for passenger services. The ship was unique in that it was the first pressured airliner. It also was the first to include an engineer as a member of its flight crew. The ships (five in total) were commandeered within two years for service when America entered World War II. It became a common theme for Pan Am, as most of its clippers were utilized for the US army. Throughout the war, Pan Am flew over ninety million miles worldwide in support of military operations.

Despite the war, the innovations and first did not stop for Pan Am. Pan Am pioneered a new air route over Africa to Iran. In 1942, it became the first airline to operate a route that went completely around the world. In 1943, Franklin D. Roosevelt became the first US president who used an airplane to travel abroad.

Chapter 5: Post World War II

After the defeat of the Axis powers by the Allies in 1945, Pan Am looked to re-establish the routes it had been servicing prior to the outbreak war, a route network that had been entirely international. By January 1946, it had reestablished itself in the Atlantic routes. Pan Am begun flying seven routes a week, from New York to Europe (five flew into London and two flew into Lisbon).

A Boeing 314 was flying into Lisbon every two weeks. Pan Am had a flight from Miami to Buenos Aires (flight time: 71 hr 15 min in a DC-3). The transpacific routes, though, were harder to salvage, as the effects of World War II disrupted Pan Am's network. After the war in the Pacific, Pan Am was not flying beyond Hawaii, though, in time, Pan Am would regain back much of this network.

Just as important as Pan Am's regaining its network were the changes being made to its airplanes. At the time, Pan Am was introducing newer and faster airplanes to its fleet every couple of years.

The Lockheed Constellation, nicknamed "Connie," was a propeller-driven airliner that was powered by four 18-cylinder radial Wright R-3350 engines that began flying transatlantic routes in 1946 for Pan Am. Connie was soon replaced in those transatlantic flights by the Stratocruiser, a Boeing 377 that was a large long range airliner that took over in 1949.

The Stratocruiser was a double-decker piston aircraft that offered sleeper seats and berths and had a lower level lounge. The Stratocruiser, for transatlantic flights, was replaced in 1952 for Pan Am by the Douglass DC6s and DC7s. These highly economical aircraft, again powered by pistons, allowed Pan Am to become the first international airline to begin economy class service on its international routes. This was done while the company expanded its international destinations. Considered to be the height of 1950s flying luxury, the Douglas DC6s and DC7s reigned in the skies until 1958 when Boeing 707 jet service was inaugurated.

The newer aircrafts were reducing travel time for the Pan Am customer, which in turn allowed for more flights for Pan Am. In January 1958, Pan American was sending 47 flights a week over the Atlantic from Idlewild. Pan Am's daily DC-7C was flying nonstop into London in 10 hours and 45 minutes. Idlewild trips to Buenos Aires were taking a little over a day. The Stratocruiser was taking passengers from California to Tokyo in around 32 hours.

1947 saw another first for the company. On June 17, 1947, Pan Am begun the first scheduled round-the-world service with Constellation L749 Clipper America. The flight originated in San Francisco and had stops in Honolulu, Tokyo, Hong Kong, Bangkok, Manila, Kolkata, Delhi, Beirut, Istanbul, Frankfurt, London, and finally New York. The flight took a week to get across the globe. The route included a change of plane initially at one of the scheduled stopovers, though when the Boeing 707 took over the route this change in the aircraft was no longer needed.

Increased Competition

During this time, Pan Am was looking to add domestic "trunk" routes to its network (connecting routes between New York and Miami as well as from New York to Chicago to California). Unfortunately for Pan Am, the airliner was denied access to these domestic routes until 1977, when deregulation occurred in the airline industry.

The denials came from the US government, who feared that the company might become a monopoly for all travel, both within the United States and abroad (ironic because the government had previously pushed for a Pan Am monopoly only a few years before).

While being denied its request domestically, Pan Am was facing trouble internationally. While Pan Am lobbied for these routes, it also made requests of the American government to remain America's major international airline. The monopoly that the American government had granted Pan Am in foreign markets, though, was failing.

Other American domestic airlines were given the right to use many of Pan Am's international routes. TWA was allowed to fly to Europe. Northwest Airlines was granted routes to Asia. United was given authorization to begin routes to Hawaii, and both Eastern & American were given routes to Mexico & the Caribbean. This access gave Pan Am competition in these markets for the first time. It found itself battling TWA in Europe, Braniff in South America, American Airlines and United Airlines for continental United States flights, and Northwest Orient in East Asia.

Pan Am Responds

To compete with its rivals, Pan Am responded as it always had, with innovation. As noted prior, Pan Am introduced the concept of "economy class" passenger service. Pan Am also invested in such advancements in the airline industry as jet aircrafts, and wide-body types.

Pan Am purchased the DC-8 and the Boeing 707, with the request from Pan Am to modify the 707 to allow for a row of six passengers instead of what had been up to then the customary five. Pan Am was also the first airliner to begin jet service across the Atlantic, flying a B707-121 (nicknamed the Clipper America) from New York to Paris on October 26, 1958.

The innovations worked. Pan Am was able to maintain a large share of the foreign market. The innovations changed the Pan Am fleet. They also changed the company's name. With the advent of the around-the-world service (a first for any airliner), Pan American Airways, Inc. was renamed Pan American World Airways, Inc.

Chapter 6: The Innovations Continue

The company, though, would not rest on its laurels. Staying ahead of the competition meant finding and using aircraft that could deliver customers quicker to their destinations. For Pan Am's bottom line, it was also important to try and put as many passengers as possible onto a given flight. The more paying customers, the more profits Pan Am could make.

With this idea in mind, Pan Am made an investment in the Boeing 747. The Boeing 747 is a wide body commercial airliner. Known as a jumbo jet, the ship was two and a half times the size of the Boeing 707. It was so large that it held the passenger capacity record for 37 years.

Pan Am was the first airliner to begin using the Boeing 747, ordering 25 of them in 1966. In 1970, the aircraft was introduced to the Pan Am fleet, to much fanfare. On January 15, 1970, First Lady Pat Nixon officially christened the first Pan Am Boeing 747 (called the Juan T. Trippe) at Washington Dulles International Airport. The ceremony included Pan Am chairman Najeeb Halaby. Instead of breaking a bottle of champagne on the aircraft (the traditional way a ship is christened) the First Lady pulled a lever that sprayed red, white and blue water on the 747.

But the promotions of the new ship did not stop there. Over the next several days, Pan Am flew the new 747s into various airports throughout the United States. The public relations effort allowed potential customers to tour the plane. A week later, regular operations of the 747 began, when Clipper Young America flew from New York to London. Problems with the engine delayed this initial departure, even resulting in the substitution of the ship. Regardless of the problems and delays, the initial flight's departure caused cheers amongst the passengers, who celebrated with champagne when the jet finally took to the air from John F. Kennedy International Airport.

The Boeing 747 was Trippe's last innovation for Pan Am. Trippe gave up presidency of the company in 1968. While he continued to attend meetings of the Board of Directors and kept an office in the company's Park Avenue office building, he no longer oversaw Pan Am's day to day operations. A visionary, his leadership, as will be seen, was to be missed in the turbulent years that lay ahead for the company.

The Supersonic Jet

As was to be expected, Pan Am kept its eye out for even faster aircrafts. In the Concorde, it thought it had found such an aircraft. Trippe himself had believed Pan Am's investment in the Boeing 747 would become obsolete for passenger travel (he believed the planes would be destined to haul cargo), figuring the planes would be replaced by faster supersonic planes.

Pan Am was one of the first of three airlines to sign options for the Concorde. However, it chose not to purchase the supersonic jet. Instead, it made an investment in the Boeing 2707, the American supersonic transport project. While the first US airline to do so, the investment in Boeing 2707 was a misstep for Pan Am, as none of these aircraft saw service after the US Congress voted against investing additional monies in the development of the aircraft.

More Improvements

Investments in aircraft were not Pan Am's only area of innovation. As Pan Am saw its traffic increasing, it found a way to set itself apart from its competition. In the early 1960s, the company commissioned IBM to build PANAMAC, a large computer that could handle both bookings for its aircraft, as well as hotel reservations. The computer, large enough that it occupied the entire fourth floor of the Pan Am building, also held such important travel information as details about the cities and countries Pan Am serviced, as well as restaurant information for Pan Am destinations.

Pan Am also upgraded its terminal at one of its main hubs, building the Worldport at John F. Kennedy International Airport in New York. Worldport held the record as the world's largest airline terminal for many years. Beautiful in design, the terminal was readily distinguishable because of its elliptical, four-acre roof, suspended from the outside columns of the terminal below by 32 sets of steel posts and cables.

The terminal was designed with the comfort of the passengers firmly in mind, as the Worldport allowed passengers to board and disembark the planes of Pan Am through the use of stairs, without the worry of getting wet, as the aircraft parked its nose under the terminal's overhang. This was an added luxury of flying Pan Am (though the introduction of the jet bridge years later made this terminal obsolete).

Pan Am recognized that customers may have issues getting out to its airports. This was especially true for those who resided in New York City (who typically did not have cars to drive to the airports). To accommodate its New York customers, starting in 1964, the airline began providing helicopter service between New York's major airports and Manhattan.

Chapter 7: A Company at its Peak

As the 1970s began, Pan Am was at the top of the international travel world. Revenue passenger traffic (in millions of passenger-miles) had grown exponentially, from 1,551 in 1951 to 8,869 in 1965 to 16,389 in 1970. The firm's advertising slogan, "World's Most Experienced Airline," seemed to be more a statement of fact then a company motto.

The company was providing scheduled service to every continent that man inhabited, with flights to as many as 160 nations. Its two main hubs were in New York and Miami. From New York City it was running operations to Europe and South America. From Miami it was handling the Caribbean.

Its service was also impeccable. It had a modern fleet. Aside from the DC-8, the Boeing 707 and 747, the Pan Am jet fleet also included Boeing 720Bs, 727s (which replaced the 720Bs), 737s, and Boeing 747SPs. These aircraft were allowing Pan Am to offer nonstop flight service from New York to Tokyo. The airline also operated Lockheed L-1011s, DC-10s, and Airbus A300s and A310s.

It also had a professional and experienced staff. Cabin crews could speak multiple languages and included many who had college degrees. The staffs made the passengers feel both at home and safe (many of them were trained as nurses).

The company began expanding. It invested in a hotel chain, the InterContinental Hotel, and a business jet, the Falcon. Both were seen as natural for a travel service company (as Pan Am saw itself). Outside of travel, the company was using its expertise in flight to create a missile-tracking range in the South Atlantic. The company also began operating a nuclear-engine testing laboratory in Nevada.

Humanitarian Work

The company, knowing the importance both of giving back to the community and the good public relations it brought, participated in several notable humanitarian flights. Pan Am operated 650 flights a week between West Germany and West Berlin during the Cold War, ensuring that the free and democratic city, surrounded by a wall built by Communist Russia, was not cut off from the rest of the war. During the Vietnam War the company also flew Rest and Recreation flights for US servicemen. These flights carried American service personnel for R&R leaves in Hong Kong, Tokyo, and other Asian cities.

Chapter 8: The Beginning of the End

Ironically, as the actions of the US government had helped build Pan Am into the company that it became, so too did that same government's actions cause its eventual demise. In the 1970s, the US government aided the Israeli military during the Yom Kippur war.

The US decision to resupply the Jewish home state infuriated the Arab world. Unable to strike back at the US militarily, the Arab nations hit the US economically, as the nations of OPEC (the Organization of Petroleum Exporting Countries) declared an oil embargo.

The 1973 energy crisis affected Pan Am in a number of ways. The oil embargo caused the price of fuel to skyrocket. The price of oil quadrupled in a year. This caused Pan Am's operational costs to go up. In addition, the energy crisis helped send the US economy into a recession.

The US consumer suddenly had less money to spend on unneeded expenses. Unfortunately for Pan Am, such an expense included travel. This helped depress demand for air travel. Adding to Pan Am's worries was an oversupply of air travel, as the US federal government began awarding more and more routes to other airlines.

As if this was not enough for the company, Pan Am also had a balance sheet problem. Pan Am had made a large investment in its fleets. It had purchased additional Boeing 747s, expecting that the demand for airline travel was going to rise in the 1970s as it had in the previous years. The company, therefore, had an asset on its books that it was not necessarily receiving revenue for.

All in all the early 1970s were disastrous for Pan Am. Many forces outside its control had hurt the company. The US government's actions in the Middle East, OPEC's oil embargo, and the resulting recession were all unfortunate occurrences for Pan AM. But there were some self inflicted wounds, notably the misreading of the air travel market. Increased costs and decreased demand helped crush Pan Am's profit margins.

Other Problems for Pan Am

The shock of the oil crisis led Pan Am to re-examine its cost structure. What the company found was a government that, it felt, was not supporting it. On September 23, 1974, a group of Pan Am employees published an ad in the New York Times to voice their displeasure over US policies that they felt were hurting Pan Am (and its bottom line). The ad cited differences in airport landing fees between nations (Pan Am was paying $4,200 to land a plane in Sydney, Australia while Qantas, an Australian airliner, was paying $178 to land a jet in Los Angeles).

The ad also cited that he U.S. Postal Service was paying foreign airlines much more than it was paying Pan Am to perform the same service of carrying US mail. The ad also raised concern about Pan Am's finance fees. The Export-Import Bank of the United States had loaned money to countries such as Japan, France, and Saudi Arabia at six percent interest rate. Pan Am, taking out loans from the same bank, was forced to pay a twelve percent rate.

Domestic Travel

Getting into domestic travel had always been the dream for Pan Am. Its founder Juan Trippe had repeatedly tried to secure such routes, and, in the 1950s, and 1960s, Pan Am attempted merger after merger (with such companies as American Airlines, Eastern Airlines, and Trans World Airlines) to acquire domestic routes. The mergers, though, never went through, and Pan Am's attempts to win the routes were repeatedly denied by the Civil Aeronautics Board. Pan Am was forced to only operate international routes (aside from the ones it had with Hawaii and Alaska).

1978 changed all of that. In that year, Congress passed the Airline Deregulation Act. The Act had two clauses. One allowed domestic carriers to begin flying internationally. The second allowed Pan Am to operate domestically.

Despite the law, only the first clause was put into effect. Other competitors convinced Congress that Pan Am would gain a monopoly on all US air routes. Once again, despite there being a law on the books, Pan Am was denied domestic routes. Worse, its competitors were now allowed to compete more and more against Pan Am in the international market.

Gaining a Foothold in the Domestic Market

In 1978 Pan Am proposed a merger with National Airlines. The move would allow Pan Am to quickly acquire domestic routes and was now legal with the deregulation of the industry. As with every other attempt by Pan Am to move into the domestic market, this one was fraught with difficulties. Two other airlines, Texas International and Eastern Airlines, began a bidding war against Pan Am, driving up the cost of the merger. Also, driving up the cost was Pan Am itself. The news that Pan Am was interested in the company drove up the price of National's stock. Still, after a review of the union by the US Justice Department for antitrust implications, the merger finally went through. Pan Am was granted authorization to buy National in 1980 in what was described by some as the "Coup of the Decade."

Almost immediately, the merger had problems. The acquisition of National Airlines at $400 million hurt Pan Am's balance sheet, which had not recovered from the large amount of purchases of Boeing 747s the company had made years earlier. The merger itself was not smooth.

The employees of National did not readily adapt to Pan Am's corporate culture. While the merger allowed Pan Am to realize an income of $4 billion in 1980 (an increase from the $2.5 billion of income realized a year prior to the merger), the integration of the two companies was poorly handled by Pan Am management, and was reflected in future years. While revenues increased 62% from 1979 to 1980, the cost of fuel went up some 157%. Other expenses classified as "miscellaneous," themselves not readily identified, increased by 74%.

As the year went on Pan Am's financial status only worsened. To shore up its losses Pan Am, under Chairman William Seawell, began selling its assets. The company first sold its 50% interest in Falcon Jet Corporation in August 1980. In November, Pan Am sold the Pan Am Building to the Metropolitan Life Insurance Company for $400 million.

The following year, in September 1981, Pan Am sold its Inter-Continental Hotel chain. During the sale of the hotel chain, Seawell was replaced by C. Edward Acker, a former executive from Air Florida and Braniff International.

Under Acker

Acker came into a bad situation. Quite simply, Pan Am was trying to force a round piece into a square hole with its National acquisition. The airline had incompatible fleets (Pan Am had L-1011s with Rolls-Royce engines, while National was using DC-10s with GE engines), mismatched route networks (National's concentrated its business in Florida), increased labor costs (part of the merger meant harmonizing the pay scales between the two companies, increasing the cost of National's operations), and, as touched on earlier, irreconcilable corporate cultures.

Acker continued Seawell's actions of selling off the company's assets. With the company facing a dire economic situation, Acker sold Pan Am's entire Pacific Division (which had 25% of Pan Am's entire route system) to United Airlines for $750 million. Pan Am later sold some of its actual fleet to other companies and countries. One such sale included Tristar airplanes to Britain, which wound up being used in the Royal Air Force.

The new chairman tried to get Pan Am a larger foothold into the domestic market. He ordered new aircraft such as the Airbus A300, A310, and A320. He then spent $100 million to purchase New York Air's shuttle service between Boston, New York City, and Washington, DC to build up the company's domestic route network.

In 1986, Pan Am bought Ransome Airlines, a commuter airline from Pennsylvania, for $65 million. Renaming it "Pan Am Express," Pan Am operated this new acquisition between New York, Los Angeles, Miami and San Diego in the United States and Berlin in Germany.

Chapter 9: Terrorism

Pan Am's iconic image (to the rest of the world it was seen as America's air carrier) made it an ideal target for terrorists. Realizing this, the airline created a security system called Alert Management Systems in 1986 to ease concerns about possible terrorist attacks and hijackings.

The new system, however, did little to improve security. As the company's financial situation worsened, the airline made cutbacks in security, justifying the action as a way not to inconvenience its passengers and lose business. The FAA fined Pan Am for nineteen security failures in one report, in 1988.

The lapses in security only hurt the company, its passengers and its crew. In 1986, Pan Am Flight 73 was hijacked in Pakistan. The terrorists would kill 20 passengers and members of the crew and would injure 120 more.

Acker was replaced by Thomas G. Plaskett, a Continental and American Airlines executive, in January 1988. Plaskett focused his energy on improving the company's on-time performance, while allowing Pan Am's security to slack. As a result, on December 21, 1988, the terrorist bombing of Pan Am Flight 103 above Lockerbie, Scotland, resulted in 270 fatalities. The consequences of these terrorist attacks were detrimental for Pan Am. Travelers feared using Pan Am, as they began associating the airline with danger.

The families of the PA103 victims filed a $300 million lawsuit against Pan Am. In response, the airline subpoenaed records of many government agencies, including the CIA, the DEA and the State Department. The subpoenaed records showed that the US government was aware of a possible bombing but did not pass the information on to the airlines (yet another instance of the US government letting Pan Am down). Still, the families claimed this to be a smoke screen--that Pan Am's lapses in security were at fault, and that Pan Am was trying to shift the blame to the US government.

The company was on a downward spiral. Even the company's once stellar customer service was beginning to suffer. Complaints of rude and unhelpful staff began to rise.

Another Sale and an Attempted Merger

In 1989, Pan Am sold its IGS (Internal German System) routes to Berlin to Lufthansa. In an attempt to dig itself out of its financial hole, Pan Am attempted another merger in that same year. In June 1989, Plaskett presented Northwest Airlines with a $2.7 billion takeover bid.

The acquisition, backed by Bankers Trust, Morgan Guaranty Trust, Citicorp and Prudential-Bache, would produce savings of $240 million due to the elimination of certain redundancies as well as the integration of certain efficiencies between the two companies. Before the deal could go through, businessmen Al Checchi presented Northwest's directors with a better deal and the directors decided to go with Checchi's merger over Pan Am's.

Gulf War

The Iraq Gulf War in 1991, which officially started with the Iraqi invasion of Kuwait in August 1990, brought transatlantic air traffic to a near stop. Pan Am could not survive. On October 23, 1990, Pan Am sold its successful London routes to United Airlines.

hese routes were Pan Am's biggest international destination, and left Pan Am with only two flights to Gatwick. This sale came a month after Pan Am announced a plan to eliminate 8.6% of its work force.

Chapter 10: Bankruptcy

With no other assets to sell and the company facing increasing deficits on its balance sheet, Pan Am was forced to declare bankruptcy on January 8, 1991. Delta Air Lines decided to buy the remaining profitable assets of Pan Am. These included Pan Am's remaining European routes and the Pan Am Worldport at John F. Kennedy International Airport. Delta also invested $100 million as a minority owner (45% share) of a reorganized and smaller Pan Am.

The plan for this new Pan Am would be to service the Caribbean, Central and South America from a hub in Miami. As part of the reorganization, the airline's creditors would hold the other 55% stake in the company. During this time, Pan Am began to move its corporate offices to Miami. Plans called for the newly organized airline to operate approximately 60 aircraft. Expectations were for the company to employ 7,500 employees and generate about $1.2 billion in annual revenues.

During this reorganization trouble began to brew. Wall Street had lost confidence in Pan Am, as the company's stock took a nose dive. The public also had doubts in the company, as potential sales for flights never materialized. With these developments, Delta itself began to lose faith in its reorganization plan.

The loss in confidence hit the company hard. Revenue shortfalls began to appear throughout October and November 1991. Delta tried to fix the damage by taking over the Boston-New York LaGuardia-Washington National shuttle service in September 1991. Delta later acquired the remaining transatlantic rights that Pan Am had possessed.

In October 1991, former Douglas Aircraft executive Russell Ray, Jr. was hired as Pan Am's new chairman and CEO. During this time, Pan Am officially moved out of its building in New York City and staff began relocating to the Miami area.

The End

But the company was beyond saving. Pan Am's senior executive team was forecasting a projected shortfall of between $100 and possibly $200 million. The company needed the final $25 million installment payment from Delta due to it at the end of November 1991 just to be able to fly through the following week. Unfortunately for Pan Am, that payment was not to come.

Delta CEO Ron Allen cut off a scheduled payment to Pan Am of $25 million (as part of its minority ownership in the company) the weekend after Thanksgiving in 1991. This cast doubt on the viability of the company. On the evening of December 3, Pan Am's Creditors Committee advised U.S. Bankruptcy Judge Cornelius Blackshear that it was trying to persuade another airline (TWA) to invest $15 million to keep Pan Am operating. Unfortunately for the company, a deal with TWA owner Carl Icahn could not be struck.

Pan Am opened for business at 9:00 am the next day and within the hour, Ray was forced to withdraw Pan Am's plan of reorganization. Ray next had to call for an immediate shutdown of operations. Pan Am officially ceased operations on December 4, 1991. 7,500 Pan Am employees, many of whom were preparing for the move to Miami, instead found themselves out of a job. Pan Am's last flown scheduled flight was Flight 436 which departed from Barbados, that day at 2 P.M. for Miami under the command of Captain Mark Pyle. Pan Am became the third major airline to shut down in 1991, following Eastern Airlines and Midway Airlines.

After only service as Pan Am's CEO for two months, Ray was replaced by Peter McHugh to oversee the sale of Pan Am's remaining assets for Pan Am's Creditor's Committee. The former company's last remaining hub, located at the Miami International Airport, was split between United Airlines and American Airlines. TWA's CEO Carl Icahn purchased Pan Am Express at a bankruptcy auction for $13 million. TWA renamed it "Trans World Express.

The Pan Am brand was sold to Charles Cobb, CEO of Cobb Partners. Cobb, along with Hanna-Frost partners, decided to invest in a new Pan American World Airways. The new company was headed by veteran airline executive Martin R. Shugrue, Jr., a former Pan Am executive with over 20 years of experience at the original carrier.

Lawsuit

Delta's decision to hold back its final payment did not go without reaction. Believing it to be a breach of contract, Pan Am Creditors Committee sued Delta for its actions for more than $2.5 billion on December 9, 1991.

A second suit was filed by a group of former Pan Am employees against Delta. In December 1995, a U.S. federal judge found in favor of Delta in both suits, reasoning that Delta could not be held liable for the fall of Pan Am.

Chapter 11: Legacy

Pan Am, at its outset, was synonymous with foreign travel. For the better part of its life, it was an ambassador of sorts for America. As such, Pan Am became ingrained into the world's psyche, and the company found a place in pop culture lure. It was the plane that, after all, brought the Beatles to America in 1964. It was the company that thief Frank Abagnale conned (and will now live on in a Broadway play and a major motion picture, both titled "Catch me if you can"). The company was a place of dreams. It established a waiting list for expected future moon flights (in fact issuing membership cards).

But perhaps nowhere will the company have a more prominent role than in the area of movies. A fictional Pan Am Space Clipper had a prominent role in 2001: A Space Odyssey.

The airline appeared in several Bond movies, and the Pan Am building was featured in Coogan's Bluff. Pan Am CEO Juan Trippe (as played by Alec Baldwin) played a significant role in the 2004 film The Aviator. The airline is mentioned in Blade Runner. It transported the Griswalds in National Lampoon's European Vacation. It gave Tony Montana, in the movie Scarface, the slogan "The World is Yours," as he got the idea from a Pan Am ad he saw

Even today, Pan Am is not far from the American mind. In 2011, ABC announced a new television series that will be based on the lives of a 1960s Pan Am flight crew. The series is called Pan Am and is expected to debut in September 2011.

The company is also important for the innovations it brought to the airline industry. It was the forerunner of transatlantic and transpacific flight. It pushed for larger aircrafts, wider aircraft. It flew the first scheduled flight around the world. It integrated air travel with hotels destinations and restaurants (a forerunner to travel agents and travel websites). It invested in jet aircrafts and computerized service. It realized the importance of customer service.

Pan Am may have suffered from bad fortune, bad management, and a government it could have felt turned its back on it. While it is gone, it can never be forgotten. The airline industry as a whole is where it is at today because of the contributions made to it by Pan Am. That is Pan Am's legacy.

CPSIA information can be obtained
at www.ICGtesting.com
Printed in the USA
LVHW081614150920
666080LV00028B/1170

9 781477 414187